To

From

Grandparents Are
Made for Hugging

"When you grow up, you should keep your grandparents
in your hearts."
Angela, age 7

Grandparents Are Made for Hugging

Children on Grandparents

David Heller
Elizabeth Heller

Villard Books New York 1993

Library of Congress Cataloging-in-Publication Data
Heller, David.
Grandparents are made for hugging: children on
grandparents/by David Heller and Elizabeth Heller.
p.   cm.
ISBN 0-679-41759-1 (alk. paper)
1. Grandparent and child—Anecdotes.   I. Heller, Elizabeth.
II. Title.
HQ759.9.H44   1993
306.874'5—dc20   92-45799

Manufactured in the United States of America
on acid-free paper

9 8 7 6 5 4 3 2

In tribute to our grandparents,
who are always in our hearts

Introduction

"Winter is on my head, but spring is in my heart," wrote Victor Hugo from the perspective of older people. Indeed, grandparents may exhibit some external manifestations of age, but their personalities and their attitudes often reveal a certain levity and lightness of spirit. As the foundation of the family, grandparents shape and influence all other family members. We can only hope that their practical wisdom and later-life playfulness rub off on the rest of us. We love them dearly because of who they are—kind and thoughtful parents and grandparents who can really tell a good story and teach us so much about life.

Grandparents and their smallest descendants have a special relationship, not only because grandparents love and appreciate children but because the feelings are mutual. And these two generations seem to share a great deal in common. Both grandparents and youngsters give high priority to family life, and both are curious about the psychological side of life in general. Both are spontaneous and unpredictable in habit and manner and are less inclined to adapt their ways to others just to conform. Most important, both are fun loving and emotionally vital; they contribute to our lives in countless ways.

We all have fond memories of our grandparents and contemporary stories too, and this book should conjure family reveries for each generation. While the book is a tribute to the special relationship between grandparents and grandchildren, parents are also frequently discussed as the children explain just how they size up the family tree.

In their lively accounts, the grandchildren have fun with these and other topics: how grandparents differ from parents, things you can do with grandparents that you can't do with parents, the most common sayings of grandparents, what grandparents can teach you, and even how most grandparents celebrate Grandparents' Day. The result is a family parade with much endearing humor, inspiration, and more than a bit of wisdom about the glorious way the generations keep marching on.

—David and Elizabeth Heller

Grandparents Are
Made for Hugging

On Why Grandparents
Are So Lovable

"They share their nachos with you . . . especially if
they get heartburn and they know you don't."
Rob, age 8

"Because their whiskers get soft and gray and are
fun to play with."
Rachel, age 7

"Grandparents are lovable because they never make
you wash the dishes."
Danny, age 8

"They say 'Let me look at you . . .' then they hug
you and pinch your cheeks and then you
hyperventilate from the whole thing."
Sheila, age 9

"Grandparents make you feel good and they never,
ever laugh at you."
Luther, age 8

"My grandparents listen to my thoughts about life
and they make me feel important."
Jacob, age 10

"Some of the best people I ever met
are grandparents."
Mandy, age 6

What Grandparents Usually Say When They First Receive Word That They Have Become Grandparents

"Thank God we don't have to toilet train these kids. . . . Their parents were tough enough."

Joyce, age 8

'

"I sure hope this child looks like our side of the family. . . . The other side all has big ears."

Henry, age 9

"Oh no, now we're really old fogies!"
Holly, age 10

"Don't you dare call me grandma, Bill. . . .
I'm not ready for that."
Heather, age 9

"I hope this baby has a guardian angel,
because he's going to need it with that
crazy son-in-law of ours."
Russell, age 10

Concerning How Most
Grandparents View Life

"They realize that the first rule in life is to not forget
your coupons when you go to the grocery store."
Luther, age 8

"They're dedicated to making other people's lives
happier . . . like their grandchildren's."
Daniel, age 9

"They think that life has got too complicated. They will tell you about the good old days when three bags of chips and soda would cost you a nickel."

Shari, age 9

"Grandparents think life is nice. . . . They aren't in a hurry to find out about the opposite of life."

Sandy, age 7

"They don't got to apologize for wanting to take it easy, so they do it every chance they get."

Julianne, age 8

"Grandparents think you should play outside a lot and get along with everybody you can, because that's what life is about."

Aaron, age 9

"My grandma says that the three most important things in life are saying your prayers, loving your family and friends, and never missing a sale at Filene's Basement store."

Jasmine, age 9

"They view life like kids do. . . . Grandparents are just older than us, but they got the same values."

Scott, age 9

"We both fall asleep around eight-thirty."
Lana, age 8

How Is a Grandparent Different from a Parent?

"The grandparents are like Santa Claus, and the parents are like Scrooge."

Shari, age 9

"Grandparents are real happy to see kids because they don't see them all the time. . . . Parents are different. They see their kids all the time."

Carey, age 7

"Grandparents have already had children, so they
are experienced. . . . Your parents might be
plain ol' rookies."
Luther, age 8

"Grandparents are willing to hang out with you
because they got time on their hands. . . . Parents
just got cooking gloves on their hands."
Danny, age 8

"Grandparents will love you even if you're
no good at school."
Malcolm, age 8

"Grandparents and children speak the same language, but all
the other people talk kinda funny."
Ally, age 9

Things You Can Do with Your Grandparents That You Can't Do with Your Parents

"Eat unlimited candy with them."
Ally, age 9

"Drink iced tea in the summer while the other people are working."
Mark, age 9

"With your grandfather, you can go hunting for deer. With your father, you can't do it because he'll just be a sap that feels sorry for the animals."
Ryan, age 9

"The older folks won't mind talkin' about what kissing is like, but the parents are too shy to talk about it with their children."
George, age 8

"Grandparents let you eat seconds on dessert, and that's why I love them."
Tammy, age 7

"You can't stay up past your bedtime with your parents. With your grandma, you can. You can watch old movies with her and Lucy Ball."
Meg, age 9

Some of the Things Grandparents Are Supposed to Do Because It's Their Role

"Tell you you're a cutey."
Annie, age 7

"They're supposed to give you great Christmas presents. They aren't supposed to hold anything back like parents are supposed to."
Danielle, age 9

"I think the ladies are supposed to bake all day.
Or maybe they just do it 'cuz they like to.
I'm not sure."
Jake, age 5

"They are supposed to kiss you and hug you and
tell you how much you have grown . . . even if they
just saw you last week."
Adam, age 8

"Grandparents are not supposed to work hard. They're supposed to live it up!"
Kasey, age 7

About How People Act When They Get to the Age of Grandparenthood

"Those older people know what they like, and they don't care about what the younger people think. . . . A kid can respect that."

Gerald, age 10

"They wear real old clothes and haircuts. They almost never wear high tops, and they might even wear stuff out of the 1960s."

Juan, age 10

"Those people got a lot of wisdom. They mostly like girls better than boys. I see it with my grandparents."

Kara, age 8

"The older people really know how to live. They fix it up so they don't have to work all day."

Butch, age 7

Common Sayings of Grandparents

" 'You need manners, you cute little devil!' . . .
Actually, my grandparents are angels and I'm
their favorite devil."
Darin, age 9

" 'You remind me of your father when he
was your age.' "
Rob, age 8

" 'I wish we could see you more often. . . . Keep telling your parents to take more vacation days.' "
Angela, age 7

" 'If you get my glasses for me, there's a quarter in it for you.' "
Danny, age 8

" 'Don't eat with your mouth open, dear. It's not ladylike.' "
Jan, age 10

" 'When I was your age, I, er . . . come to think of it, I can't remember it when I was your age.' "
Vernon, age 9

" 'Have some more ice cream. It's good for you.' "
Marie, age 7

" 'There's no fool like a young fool.' "
Aaron, age 9

" 'If it was up to me, I would let you skip school
and we could go fishing.' "
Jerome, age 9

"We got the same relatives in between us."
Diana, age 9

A Few of the Many Things That Grandparents and Grandchildren Have in Common

"We both like to give hugs. . . . Grandparents are made for hugging."

Simone, age 9

"We love them and they love us. . . . It's an even deal."

Jan, age 10

"Both the children and the grandfathers like to smell things before they eat them."

Phil, age 7

"The older people and the kids both like chewing gum, but it might be harder for the older people. . . . Maybe they should have used more toothpaste."

Irene, age 8

"A good grandparent tells you hilarious stories about what goofballs your parents used to be."

Russell, age 10

What Makes a Person a Good Grandparent?

"Have jelly beans with you all the time."
Mitch, age 6

"You should be able to run about four miles, so you keep up with your grandson."
Daniel, age 9

"To be a good grandparent, you should
look like an owl."
Maureen, age 9

"Owning plenty of vitamins. They got to have pep
so they don't run out of gas when you play
cards with them."
Rob, age 8

"Having a lot of potato chips on the coffee table.
You got to be ready if you got kiddies coming over."
Megan, age 8

Ways That a Grandma or Grandpa Can Make a Kid Feel Special

"Money can get the message to you."
Darin, age 9

"Grandparents can tell you they love you and they really hate your cousins, but they aren't supposed to say anything about it."
Shari, age 9

"They make you feel special by saying that you look pretty even if you just have a T-shirt and jeans on. . . . They go mostly by the face."

Simone, age 9

"They make your favorite food, which in my case is grandma's fried chicken."

Bruce, age 9

"They always give you a purple birthday card because they know it's your favorite color."

Susanna, age 9

"They kiss you on your head and on your ears."

Alissa, age 4

"They like to play and talk and laugh. They're like kids. . . .
Grandparents are just like kids with gray hair."

Christine, age 9

What Are Your Own Grandparents Like?

"They are like me but nicer."
Phil, age 7

"They sleep a lot, but I used to too."
Gina, age 6

"They both have snowy hair."
Francine, age 7

"My grandparents are funny; my parents are real serious. So I have to be loose and figure out which ones are calling the shots."

Jeffrey, age 10

"They are pretty short. Maybe they didn't used to be."

Todd, age 6

"They fuss all the time with each other because they are mostly old lovebirds."

Angela, age 7

"I love them and hope that I can take them with me when I grow up and have a family."

Sylvia, age 8

"My grandma can read people's minds. . . . She always
knows when I want to eat."

Judd, age 6

What Makes Your Own Grandparents Unique?

"They are very loving people, and they know
how to spell."
Earvin, age 6

"My grandparents are special grandparents because
they still have hair."
Tamara, age 7

Typical Things That Children Request from or Say to Their Grandparents

" 'Can I move in with you? You have
less rules here.' "
Todd, age 6

" 'I hope God blesses you and me because we love
each other. The other people in the family like my
brother are on their own.' "
Christine, age 9

" 'Grandma, how do you stay so pretty? Maybe
Grandpa should do what you do.' "
Danielle, age 9

" 'Grandma, Grandpa, come quick! There's
teeth in this jar!' "
David, age 7

" 'Grandpa, have you snored all your life? Or did it
hit you when you got to be a grandpa?' "
Josiah, age 8

Concerning the Great Wisdom
of Grandparents

"They get their wise ideas from all that old-fashioned
tea they drink."
Aaron, age 9

"If you're a little boy, they tell you that you
shouldn't look at ladies yet because your eyes will
pop out. . . . They have that kind of
real-life wisdom."
Arnold, age 10

"Grandparents get wise because they learn from the mistakes they made in bringing up their children. . . . It's kinda like trials and errors."

Al, age 10

"It must be that wisdom just comes to you when you are about sixty. . . . You don't have to do anything special to get it."

Susanna, age 9

"Grandparents have a lot of experience and they aren't shy about reminding you about it."

Harmon, age 8

"They have lived for years and years, so they know all about life. Like how many cookies will give you a stomachache. They're real smart."
Lynn, age 8

"Grandparents get their wisdom from heaven, but they get love from their families right here on earth."
Simone, age 9

"My grandparents showed me where they live on a map, but I can't drive there myself yet because I don't know how . . . and there's a river in the way too."

Judd, age 6

What Have You Learned from Your Grandparents?

"Not to eat off the floor. There could be vegetables down there."
Julia, age 8

"The world is a great place, and there was a day when there wasn't even any planes or cars, so don't forget that we are making a lot of progress."
Al, age 10

"They teach you how to stay married a long, long time . . . even if you get a little bored with each other once in a while."
Maria, age 8

How Grandmothers and Grandfathers Are Alike and How They Are Different from Each Other

"One of them is usually bald, and one of them isn't."
Bart, age 9

"My grandma looks like a fresh apple. My grandfather don't look like no fruit. He looks more like a vegetable."
Arnold, age 10

"My grandparents were neighbors of Abraham Lincoln
or else they knew him."
Jonathan, age 6

"Grandmas smile more. Grandpas complain more when you don't put on their television shows."
Maxie, age 8

"I think that grandmothers might live longer, probably because they don't eat so many steaks and cholesterol food."
Brett, age 10

"Grandfathers always watch their budgets, but grandmas don't care about silly things like that."
Angela, age 7

"Grandparents like to hold hands a lot and look real gooey eyed at each other. I hope I'm not a grandparent for a long, long, long time."
Michael, age 9

Expert Observations About Grandmothers

"Grandmothers especially love children. They even
like to baby-sit kids named Junior."
Daniel, age 9

"They sure do sleep a lot."
Luther, age 8

"Grandmas like to get extra bubble gum out of the machines without putting in another dime."
Lloyd, age 6

"They teach you all the family secret recipes, but they got them all memorized because it would be too dangerous to write them down."
Megan, age 8

"When you go to my grandfather's house, he'll push you in a
wheelbarrow when he's working in the yard. . . . He does
crazy stuff like that, so that's why I love him."

Josiah, age 8

Noteworthy Traits of Grandfathers

"They always sit down and pull their pants up and
then turn on wrestling."
Sheila, age 9

"Some of them go to California and smoke
pipes there."
Blake, age 7

"You can read the newspaper together with your
grandfather out on the porch—as long as
you can read."
Carey, age 7

"Grandfathers help you build a model airplane, but then they get so excited about it they hardly let you do any of it."

Brad, age 9

"My grandpa tells me stories about how Peter Rabbit and his family live in his cabbage patch, but I don't believe him because there's too many bugs and crawlers outside for anybody to live out there."

Judd, age 6

"Grandpas kiss you good night and tuck you in real good so no boogeymen can get you while you're asleep."

Allison, age 6

Cards to Grandma or Grandpa

To My Grandparents,
Have a good day and don't slip on any of those pies
that are laying around on the kitchen floor.
Love,
Daniel, age 9

Dear Grandma,
I love you even more than the Care Bears.
Love,
Kathleen, age 6

Dear Grandma,
Your cooking is great. Why didn't you ever teach
my mom to cook?
From,
Rob, age 8

Dear Grandpa,
Please talk to my mom. She won't let me smoke a
pipe. I told her if it was good enough for you it was
good enough for me, too. Women—they just don't
understand us men.
Russell, age 10

Dear Grandma,
Please send some of your spaghetti in the mail. I
miss eating it a lot.
Love,
Angela, age 7

Dear Grandma and Grandpa,
Here is a picture of my garden vegetables.
Love,
Jenna, age 6

P.S. There aren't any pictures here because my
garden didn't do so good.
The worms ate them all up.

Dear Grandpa,
Please stop calling me "Shorty."
It's going to give me a complex.
Thanks,
Luther, age 8

Things That Grandparents Collect

"All of the grandparents try to collect as much money as they can, since that security money they get isn't that much."
Luther, age 8

"They collect old stories and they tell you them until you are blue all over your face."
Tommy, age 8

What Do Grandparents All Over the World Have in Common?

"Grandchildren who love them."
Corinne, age 10

"Grandkids who wished they lived closer to them."
Danny, age 8

"They've all been married for a hundred years."
Angelo, age 7

"By the time they get to their age, they should have
lost all their prejudices and figured out it was
a waste of time."

Jolita, age 10

"They're sick and tired of all the wars. But they can't
get it through to the younger people that they
should put a stop to it."

Sammy, age 9

"Most grandparents like to take walks by the
water . . . even the ones who never
go swimming."

Rob, age 8

"They all are real caring and loving to their
grandchildren no matter what country they live in."

Simone, age 9

"They all take Greyhound bus tours and go all around the country having fun."

Jacob, age 10

"All grandparents spoil their grandchildren . . . but I'm not going to tell anybody I said this."

Megan, age 8

"They all make you sit straight at the table. They're fanatics about it, but their food is good, so all the grandchildren go along with it."

Aaron, age 9

"All grandparents save their pennies and bring them to the bank and tell the bank people not to cheat them."

Al, age 10

When a Person Grows Up,
What Can He or She Do
to Make Sure Grandma
and Grandpa Are Remembered?

"Make sure that you tell your own children how much fun you had with your grandparents, like the times they took you to the pond."

Daniel, age 9

"Tell the new people in the family about the time Grandma put salt instead of sugar in some cookies she was making, because she didn't have her glasses on."

Serena, age 8

Why God Set Things Up
So That We Have Grandparents

"So we always have somebody nice to visit
on the holidays."
David, age 7

"They are like substitute teachers, but you know
them better. If your mother is sick, they fill in and
cook you up a storm."
Sheila, age 9

"Grandparents might even be wiser than kids,
or maybe it's a tie."
Devon, age 8

"So you have somebody to stay with when your
parents take a kissing cruise."
Josiah, age 8

"God created grandparents to make sure there was
someone in every family who spoiled all
the kids rotten."
Kirby, age 9

"I think there was two grandparents on Noah's ark. When the water cleared, they probably opened a retirement place for older people."

Jackson, age 10

"God made grandparents just in case your parents can't take care of you anymore. They're kinda like insurance."

Kristi, age 9

"God created grandparents when He was making all of the really good people."

Lane, age 9

DAVID HELLER, Ph.D., is a leading authority on children and their views of the world. He has authored a number of successful books on the subject, including *Love Is Like a Crayon Because It Comes in All Colors, My Mother Is the Best Gift I Ever Got, Fathers Are Like Elephants Because They're the Biggest Ones Around, Dear God: Children's Letters to God, The Children's God,* and "*Growing Up Isn't Hard to Do If You Start Out as a Kid.*" His work with children has been featured all across the country, including segments on *20/20* and CNBC, and articles in *People, Parents, Good Housekeeping, Redbook, USA Today, Psychology Today, Parenting,* and in nationally syndicated pieces for Universal Press Syndicate. He graduated from Harvard and the University of Michigan, and has taught at both.

ELIZABETH HELLER, M.S., has assisted on all the previously mentioned books and has co-authored a forthcoming one about children and Christmas. She has developed a children's news program for cable TV and produced and hosted a radio show for children on WBZ in Boston. As Director of Public Relations for Catholic Charities, she worked extensively for children and children's charities. She holds a bachelor's degree in English from Santa Clara and a master's degree in journalism from Boston University.